# Back of A Vast

*Also by Mark Goodwin*

Else

# Back of A Vast

## Mark Goodwin

Shearsman Books
Exeter ·

First published in the United Kingdom in 2010 by
Shearsman Books Ltd
58 Velwell Road
Exeter EX4 4LD

www.shearsman.com

ISBN 978-1-84861-119-1
First Edition

# Contents

**Distance a Sudden**
My Warm Bedding Cools to Moor                          11
A Bout of Walking                                     12
Borrowdale Details                                    14
Kynance Guessed                                       15
Dark Bird with Corner                                 17
Zy Skennor                                            19
Torridon Peopled                                      20
M Alta                                                21
Shedding                                              22

Twilight Run                                          25
Rail Move *I*                                         26
Feathery Archetexture, A Lincoln Cathedral            28
Rurban Membrane, A Sheffield Rim, North East          29
Moor on Paper Under Foot                              31
A Worth                                               43
Slake                                                 46
Two Llynnau, Moelwynion                               51
Mortals Through Gogarth                               53
Mont Blanc Away                                       56
On Blhà Bienn, Skye, January 1st 2002                 57
Peop Tor Ridon Led                                    59
Dawlish Corner                                        60

**Ish Coast Etched**
Zennor Sky                                            65
On The Zennor Field Path, A West Penwith              66
On The Zennor Field Path, A West Penwith II           68
Zy Nor Sken                                           73

Passing Through Sea Thorn                              76
Aromomentic Lo(r)cation, Andaluvia                    79
Aromatic Seira Tejeda, Andalucía                      81
Voltage                                               84
Star Frost, A Corie Làir, A Strath Carron             85


Acknowledgements                                      89

*for Chris, and for Brian*

# DISTANCE A SUDDEN

## My Warm Bedding Cools to Moor

but I am not unsheltered    nor chilled    this little
bothy condenses    its weight    of stone blocks

wooden beams    slate tiles    the bothy clings to
land under wind    it is bravery    in it & from in it

my body & heat spread    peacefully out to the sweet
danger    my arms & legs    stretch    kilometres in an

instant some me    grows    as a slow map    sleepiness
pulls    my heat to laser through    shadows expands

my confines    to concentrate distances    reeds tussocks
rocky knolls winter red    -twigged birches black peat

-water dried grasses snow    -silvered ridges & mountain
flanks icicles moon behind    speedy whisps of frayed

sky faint    platinum lochans cliffs white    twirling strands
& filaments    of streams steaming falls all    spread through

my bedding stretch    my flesh &    bones    wide & tight
through & across    miles of wild ground around    this

foetal house I    drift    my stillness in

## A Bout of Walking

original abroad    aboriginal step    from manicured

Oz's    track to    preserved Native Australian    hands
blown on stone    red or black    smokey edges    behind
an iron cage    I into the rockery    of/for    snake-song

& spidery venom    eve light is a grease on eucalypts
light    edges the ages so    ages vibrate brand new    I
am careful to    leave    clues for my return    this cracked

landscape of granite blocks is labyrinth    I leave a giant
burnt matchstick above the wall    back    to modern time
a big thick singed twig    how the mouth of fire has spoken

here:    yelled    up    against distant cities where whites
tremble    in black dreamtime    dark roos boing    away
like energetic    monks genuflecting repeatedly to    distance

I see how such land gives    birth    to aboriginal imagi
nations    Geriward ground now ever kissing Victoria's
amused skin    pulling    bones up to sunlight like    fresh

green shoots for    fire    I am alone as Sun    flattens hot
egg across wide sky-ground    sinks into ground-sea    Moon
but my nape is home to count    less barefoot    dancers

travelling like water    white drops of paint spatter on    me
laughter    well    milked cairns sag    peopled faces    creased
as granite beards    thick & black as night    time    eucalypts

this    whole    Geriward garden rockery portraits brains    lit

## Borrowdale Details

soft larch needles    I sniff wish    thin dangling larch twigs hold
raindrops    christ & pagan wrapped to tinsel    autumn light
has projected Borrowdale's matter    a work crafts growth    I

peer    at a twig's knuckles    a needle's green edge    a tiny globe
dissolving landscape    Borrowdale is a    mass    of details full
a vastness of minuscule    high    resolution beauty    immense

numbers of bits    of leaf-frames pebbles daddylongleg claws
for an instant I spread    let    a moment explode    as I climb
through woods by crags    every detail of me    follicle bone-cell

grease    shatters or slicks    amongst    Borrowdale's infinite
tiny details    one    of my gasps stretches wetly with the beck
others entwine with white fibres of gills    unravelling    gravity

the calcium atoms of my teeth    jumble    along drystone walls
moss green-gleaming    my meal    of Herdwick meat    passes
through my gut whilst Borrowdale's    details    digest my soul

## Kynance Guessed

a cup of   sea   please a ship   slips a window
pane   fractured triangular pillars   Asparagus

Bishop Gull Bellows   sail-line-white wrinkles
rising to tidal cream-brown rising   to black sea

-cleaned Serpentine rising   to must   ard green
lichen & a silvery   sea-gull-shit-streak   frayed

Lizard's gentle   torments torment   il heath   er
louse   wort yel   low rattle   hissy clatter of sud

den drizzle pas   sing to darken a pebble   a cup
of sea I sip at land's serrated edge a ship   slips

glass a pane of tight   sea smooth clear between
teeth   -white mullions a horizon   is miniature in

crystal bending a tempt   sea at   emptsea a cup
of sea spills past white-painted window latches

smears its spacey glass I swig   a container ship's
squeaks   its wet finger across a horizon's clean

pane a massive   fly crawls over a ship's needle
bow I wake   in a cup of curveless   glass as a

shiny wake of    scratches an in    coming tide's
people a so    aked mass of straggling beliefs I sip

at sea smiles frowns laughter tears slowly fill a
cove cover over our    pebbles are under people

see    through humans    bending light letting words
evolve like    fish an in    coming tide's city of

wobbling buildings fl    owing over s    ands and
Serpentine    rock's child's    smacked hand mag

nified down to imp    acting aeons in a cup of sea
scolds if spilled on flesh's forge    tting a horizon

's ship is as sharp    eye-grit night will    blink again
st but for now day's blue inflates    a warship's grey

prongs & whale car    case hull make agreements
with a cup of sea in which I'm ship-shape dropping

a teaspoon    anchor my face    reflected in it it shat
ters my glass inter    i    or with the tiniest vast clunk

## Dark Bird with Corner

a rim of a ravine draped    with moss
& heather  a chough?    a dark clotted

part    of air her *crock-crock* a    beauty
full    breaking of sleek    sky

-flesh into jagged    elsewheres    a writhe
of a burn's rubbing rock greased

with sea-bottom greens    primeval
evidence    water as melted    mind ever

falling brain-white    thoughts of clouds
running electrically across ground

and    down crags a raven's finger
-feathers flutter like a pianist's strangest

dream white    water    fall-lines with
auroras of hiss-mist    behind tangled

birch trunks & leafless    branches inky
-slick claws black grappling    hooks

sure    of nothing a    moor running from
a chasm's lips into    distance a sudden

drop abhorrent    to a ground's khaki
uniform of tussocky bog    openness routed

by intricate    enclosure a ravine a    corner
of a    world funnelling    reverie at a

back of a vast    stage An Teallach a mass
of ground's applause & roar    solidified

she rolls her *crock-crock* reply to my are
you a raven?    parcels her slippery

blue black    twirls downside up flight
moment hangs    shiny soot hands of air

a sequin eye    inspects    our bright
Gore-tex-wrapped    shapes her dark    sharp

in our eyes    unfathomable gladness    a vole
trickles over snow    swift as sorrow some

very    small glass    & metal room of our car
parked below    is dead to dreaming    move

meant a feathered throat    & beak scrapes
the    in    visible corner    a


                    cross close sky




Note: *An Teallach* is a mountain in Wester Ross;
its name means *The Forge*.

## Zy Skennor

trans    lucent purr    ple pink guernsey cows graze
lit silver grass    Zennor sky smashed to    peace

on mead    ow! at forty thousand feet    a corn
ish coast etched    in steam moments    merm    aid

scale wisps    ers soft granite out    crops ancest    or
ash tree living in through round    a ruined cott    age

of sky's gold    oranges & silver    streamers a sky's
insides inside a gurnard's guts a    vast    pub of

coloured gusts & mist musicians jamming cumuli
-guitars-cirrus-chords-voices-accordian-anvils buttery

sky-milk    dribbles twilight mines    plum    met deep
through heavens' rippling    ringing tin    song gone

## Torridon Peopled

scree's broken   words   grate & clatter   our boots punc
tuate travel the   slip   of stone over stone of   frozen
spears doors bullets of   ground   ice   feathers tangling

white strands on   philosophies of cold a   foothold of
silvery solid   worth   warm gold the sun   plates slabs
with frail light under   ice-skin over glacis water wriggles

black   gurgles downwards like tadpoles under cellophane
east wind twists   Siberian thoughts   into our skin   our
fingers tinder   set   alight with ice whilst   indoors invades

our centres with its distant mass as all this Highland vast wraps
us with   open   our day is a gap of light cracked   in winter's
stone night we rush   through we   turn   from hard iced

rocks & blade air we   descend   to the valley's waiting hol
low shapes   frozen moss & yellowed grasses   cup our steps
with soft crunches   as the light drinks   it   self   dry & dim

a crowd   of birch saplings knee & waist high are a   people
we walk amongst   I touch   their twig-ends   so   the slender
map lines   they   make vibrate like memories   on   fire but


Note: *Torridon* is a village, a loch and a range of mountains
in Wester Ross. *Torridon* is Gaelic for *Place of Transference*.

## M Alta

soft yell    ow lime    stone whiles away pow
dery faces across a pre    -historic    altar chisel

-dimples rain dry    s    till    ness a voltage of liz
ard repeats hot cruci    fixes its    shadows an

alphabet of b    urnt twigs a fig    -tree's leaves
cup its figs a street-    cat falls to    bits in the sun

re-beg    ins in a shadow in    a harbour's depth
can    non balls & man    gled aircraft rust to shy

fragments of moon a vast    f    lag of sea    f    laps
cracks rips    against razor coast pert    on a jeep's tail

gate a watermelon    unexploded holds    its wet waits
for a mouth to det    onate capers    stiffen between

the sun's lips an olive    -tree's pocked & contorted
trunk    s    lips the bones of a knight in    to yellow

p    odour

## Shedding
*for Janet*

wearing the warm wind    wearing away

at me wearing at   some   way the oldest
rocks   Hornstone printing into   my back

-skin the wind's   warm torn voices   roll
in my ears guttural but spacious rush hush

weaving my brain   's surface to rippling salt
y see the wind's   empty shiatsu hands   loll

my head my   face   a dish to the sun   fill
ing with light's collected distance   Leicester

in its bowl below   Bradgate high   g   round
as majestic as Sydney today   soft September

glints   a mother-board processing people   my
eyes close over now wearing   the warm wind

tears on   my skin tears   at my skin the wind
rooting up my nostrils rips   off my face over

& over &   over   again my mask   stretched
with   the wind my skin   a flapping flag ever

lengthening the    wind copies    my expressions
over    &    over carries    copies of my    miles

down an old land copies    of off    my face my
bones & meat & guts all bl    own over rove

out & out &    out a    cross hope's vast digesting
space    like leaves leaving the oak trees    face

                flung to    air all    ways

## Twilight Run

the light pulls at my footprints my
bones gently jolt on light cool sweat I clear
air barriers I curve
past winter trees' slow twirls 3d spin-linger I am solid among
lit spirits defined
trees' spaces this race again
against my flesh & a world goes well & first sadness falls
out of my soles I leave
a track of where & breath a future the line
of my route cuts
the world in two but keeps my & it complete look
of the sun's sink call
of feet to ground mucus coughed up & spat is
proof to grass I keep
the running through this light muscles lively among ghosts' twirls
of bare-leaved trees write
with my motion parallax is a flesh through world

# Rail Move *I*

worlds   flick you open   wheat fields   worlds in
cinema in cinema worlds   distant pop   lars along

rails of worlds through you   close in to gritstone
blocks & blue bricks   window fr   ames flick you

thick   hawthorn-clad em   bankment bulging in
carriages film you open out   to a sm   ear of summer

flood over grass   you are in window frames   in be
yond   are six thick   steaming cigarette stubs stick

ing up from an ashtray of power station   is cinema
carriages? cinema window along   grey flick-clat

ter of rail   ings blurring   orange-brick squat pitch
ed-roofed blocks   you are in   gravel piles smashed

ground curled cables wire   scritches flick   you along
sidings   tar-st   icky sleepers stacked like melting Kit

Kats   train frames worlds open out   to thistle-clogged
meadow   you cin   ema &   an ancient hedgerow's dis

closures   of three d wooden alphabet obscured by sum
mer's froth of momentary foli   age train-frames through

world a sudden    black splashing & spray of starlings rails
along you a nearly-neon    green-striped field & glossy

black blobs of plast    ic-wrapped silage you    are in flick
-worlds close in to    a row of dead willows'    white ghost

less bones    train carriages window along    nine back gard
ens    flashed past but each    as distinct & familiar as a

dreamt stranger    cinema film frames through open to    a
river's smooth seen sound below a hillside cascade    of win

dows roofs & chimneys    you along you in window    close
in to a cut    ting through red cracked rock entangled with pre

-historical smiles of ivy    world's carriages flick rails    deep
close in    to bright inside reflection you    window film cinema

as    a black of tunnel passes your face away from one split
place to a next and you're gone along frames you are re

placed rails frame you by grazing cows train film flick as black
& white as snow & coal and as small as    jewellery    you a

train    train you    you through

### Feathery Archetexture, A Lincoln Cathedral

sun sinks through earth's    skin a cathedral's
buttresses    flap    si    lently    still as bells'

bongs slowed through dream    to hoots two
wide round North    & South eyes let    light

        from nigh    t    in

## Rurban Membrane, A Sheffield Rim, North East

scarp    along Don's arc shall    ow hanging
loops of pow    er-line    pylons    dull silvery
frames holding    dead space live    to shock oak

leaves pat drips & drop    rain through fractal
cascades of tiny tile-glistens    water smear slip
slide trickle fall here is    a pas    (s)age a place of

passing    a band-land a rim full    of reverie's
solid switches a circuit    where hopes in sol
ution show    their ghosts through    forms of

solidity found    here trea    sures of detritus for
cent    ripetal/    fugal souls DANGER    OF
DEATH beside    a cobweb droo    py with rain

drops sag    ging rung-loops han    ging wob
bly glass globes fresh    webs of barbed    *xxx*
-wire barbed-wire-    wrapped    *xxxxxxxx*

girders    jagged tinsel met    allic Christ-crowns
wet-in    sect-wing-buzz    moist-rattle-hiss as
electromagnetic static comes off cable just sixty

feet up my skeleton's    aerial sheathed in meat
directly be    low spine tingle-tight & test    icles
vibrant I'm a passage for a subtle invasive freight

jaw-muscles' unseen ne    on tension like word-urge
just halted through    shadow-green gaps in leaf-froth
a lost cemetery jumps out com    ical as Hammer

Horror if    not for the shock of    lost loss    graves
em    braced by ivy stone    engraved with decor
ative plant-forms & chis    elled words which begin

grief's distance touched by i    vy's thousands of
exp    loring hands rows    of gravestones to    tally
enveloped in    growth in pelts    of vegetation

green-flesh figures with stone    cores in dim drip
ping musky under-leaf of feral    belief's a robin's
eye a tiny dark hole with a speck of    light oaks

standing round pay rain through their leaves as last
respects from wild    erness a glimp    sed wren like a
word on the tip of no()w()here's    tongue tree roots

remem    bering human dead humans effort    lessly
with buried effort for    get a wire branch of an Eng
land's power-grid    passes hisses close    conveys

energy to away    water    fresh from sky run    nels
slowly along little channels of chiselled let    ters in
stone prayers under    foliage    water reading no

thing read    god's grey ear of driz    zle-mist presses
closer to ground to hear    a va    pour ear between up
& down between across &    close between coming

       & g    one

## Moor on Paper Under Foot

map tight in its Ortlieb droplets
spattered like miniature mag

nifying glasses trembling water
-domes bending print on

paper the big blue 81 northing
the loops of its eight threaded

through by the thick orange 350
contour and just above this

northing's eight in an old-eng
lishy script is the letter m end

ing field system a blanket of
ground bordered so contained

by the big A625 & thin brown
B6521 Owler Tor a Red Bull

can stuffed in a crack a crisp
packet full of rain pick it up it

drips see-through snack Nation
al Trust FB weir MP spot

-height 301 green dashes stit
ched close to Burbage Brook's

blue silk filament double-arrow
pines green wash neat print

ed lobed bulbs signifying trees
that lose their leaves when

Persephone goes back below
CRoW Act access-arrows bri

stle-cluttered like purple shark's
teeth screwed to grit a bronze

Longshaw Estate plaque den
ted by stones having been

smashed into it but its bent
damage now belongs

matches some gritty Vandal &
Goth romance drinking hot

red current in Mother Cap's
eastern lee as hail wasps past

white pellets gather in ground's
creases lace-frilling hori

zontal corners formed between
gritstone & moorgrass mass

ive purple cloths of storm scene
ry pulled on wind sun-blur

foundering in depths of late
afternoon a cluster of high

cloud-edges scrolled in silver slow
ly erased by red-grey-blue

chiffon the place boulderers call
Secret Garden full of hand

-hold fruits & blooms for feet all
eroded from compacted part

icles washed down from what
was aeons later named Scotland

a playing place with cream black
-striped filaments of birch trem

bling as a fabric of weather directs
their performing Burbage

Rocks is gun-metal pastel smudged
under winter's finger (think

of summer's touch climbing a crisp
focus on intricately written

architecture) the A625 purple on
paper dog-legged between

Toad's Mouth & Burbage Bridge
a rain-glossed asphalt sliding

headlights amongst twilit heath
ery grit textures a conduit for

pods holding humans insulated
from world by revolving rub

ber Hathersage Moor sheepfold rain
gauge cairns spot-height 384

Winyards Nick Over Owler Tor's
wet crepuscular rocks a cong

regation of fossilised birds
perched on forever whilst be

low owlstone grit the big bibles
of Millstone's walls unseen

from here but felt as an inevitable
sudden dropping into imagine

the heather as a roarin' o' waves
tumblin' o'er a world's end just

below the big blue northing 82 up
around the 400 contour looking

up at The Rasp E2 5b on Higgar
Tor's leaning rock god brow thou

shalt not engrave strands of rain
dripping sideways heart a mill

stone suddenly molten December
algae glowing greasily the imp

ulse to climb here a sullen lust fall
ing from throat to intestines thr

ough thighs to stuck-still feet sud
den shush as wind stops on pass

ing below the 350 contour between
Carl Wark & Burbage Brook pines

softly watchful through falling
light brush skin across slick

transparent mapcase smear wet over
smooth for rough ground loud

under Vibram soles body nude just
under a border of Gore-tex be

tween weather's directions a be
ing be    neath its own thumb on

paper may()be intrinsically in
volved with else's where two grouse

urgle round ground's ear

▲

## Moor Map End Gleans

1.

droplets mag water on northing threaded
350 this eng end of contained brown Bull

crisp it Nation spot    stit Brook's arrow
print trees when below bri shark's bronze

den been bent belongs    & hot Cap's past
ground's hori between mass scene blur

late high slow blue    call hand all part
what Scotland black trem directs Burbage

smudged think    crisp written on between
Bridge sliding heath for insulated rub rain

384 Tor's cong birds be bibles unseen
inevitable imagine    waves just up looking

Higgar thou rain mill    December imp fall
thr sud pass be    tween pines falling slick

over loud just be    be on in    grouse ear


2.

threaded bull
arrow bronze

past blur
part Burbage

between rain
unseen looking

fall slick ear

3.

bull bronze
blur Burbage
rain looking ear

4.

bronze Burbage ear

▲

## Moor on Paper Under Foot #2

map tight in its Ortlieb
droplets spattered like miniature magnifying glasses
trembling water-domes bending print on paper

the big blue 81 northing
the loops of its eight threaded through
by the thick orange 350 contour
and just above this northing's eight
in an old-englishy script is the letter m
ending field system

a blanket of ground bordered so contained
by the big A625 & thin brown B6521
Owler Tor
a Red Bull can stuffed in a crack
a crisp packet full of rain
pick it up it drips see-through snack

National Trust
FB
weir
MP
spot-height 301
green dashes stitched close
to Burbage Brook's blue silk filament
double-arrow pines
green wash
neat-printed lobed bulbs signifying trees
that lose their leaves when Persephone goes back below

CRoW Act access-arrows bristle-cluttered
like purple shark's teeth
screwed to grit a bronze Longshaw Estate plaque
dented by stones having been smashed into it
but its bent damage now belongs
matches some gritty Vandal & Goth romance

drinking hot red current in Mother Cap's
eastern lee as hail wasps past
white pellets gather in ground's creases
lace-frilling horizontal corners formed between
gritstone & moorgrass

massive purple cloths of storm-scenery pulled on wind
sun-blur foundering in depths of late afternoon
a cluster of high cloud-edges scrolled in silver
slowly erased by red-grey-blue chiffon

the place boulderers call The Secret Garden
full of hand-hold fruits & blooms for feet
all eroded from compacted particles
washed down from what was aeons later named Greenland

a playing place with cream black-striped filaments of birch
trembling as a fabric of weathers directs their performing

Burbage Rocks is gun-metal-pastel smudged
under winter's finger
(think of summer's touch
climbing a crisp focus on intricately written architecture)

the A625 purple on paper dog-legged between
Toad's Mouth & Burbage Bridge
a rain-glossed asphalt sliding headlights amongst
twilit heathery grit textures
a conduit for pods holding humans insulated
from world by revolving rubber

Hathersage Moor
sheepfold
rain gauge
cairns
spot-height 384
Winyards Nick

Over Owler Tor's wet crepuscular rocks
a congregation of fossilised birds perched on forever
whilst below owlstone grit the big bibles of Millstone's walls
unseen from here but felt as an inevitable sudden dropping
imagine the heather as a roarin' o' waves
tumblin' o'er a world's end

just below the big blue northing 82 up around the 400 contour
looking up at The Rasp, E2 5b, on Higgar Tor's leaning rock-
        god-brow
thou shalt not engrave
strands of rain dripping sideways
heart a millstone suddenly molten

December algae glowing greasily
the impulse to climb here a sullen lust
falling from throat to intestines
through thighs to stuck-still feet

sudden shush as wind stops on passing below
the 350 contour between 𝕮𝖆𝖗𝖑 𝕸𝖆𝖗𝖐 & Burbage Brook
pines softly watchful through falling light

brush skin across slick transparent mapcase
smear wet over smooth
for rough ground loud under Vibram soles
body nude just under a border of Gore-tex

between weather's directions a being
beneath its own thumb on paper
maybe intrinsically involved with else's where

two grouse gurgle round ground's ear

▲

## Moor Map End Gleans #2

1.

Ortlieb glasses    paper northing
through contour eight    m system

contained B6521    Tor crack rain
snack Trust FB weir MP 301

Close filament pines wash trees
below cluttered teeth    plaque

it belongs    romance Cap's past
creases between moorgrass

wind afternoon silver chiffon
Garden feet particles    Greenland

birch performing smudged finger
touch architecture between

bridge amongst textures
insulated rubber Moor sheepfold

gauge cairns 384    Nick rocks forever
walls dropping waves end contour

brow engraven sideways molten
greasily lust intestines feet below

Brook light    mapcase smooth soles
Gore-tex being paper where ear


2.

northing system
rain close

trees plaque
past moorgrass

chiffon Scotland
finger between

textures sheepfold
forever contour

molten below
soles ear


3.

system close
plaque moorgrass

Greenland between
sheepfold contour

below ear


4.

close grass between contour ear

## A Worth

December a Chat    sworth's frost
is private    keep(s)    out we    sneek

through a weak    ness cross    an e
state wall go    through a bro    ken

down gap where    badg    ers pass
and some    people tresp    ass

we enter slants    of late light man
gling in red bracken    sun's win

ter membranes pla(y)    ting mass
ive fat oaks    golden & ground    glist

ening pale pink where f    rost uttered
water to delicate    solid we    climb

an oak-peopled hillside through nar
ratives escaped from dark    German

ic woods but lit    by late beyond-noon
light in an En    gland dreamt a little

stream's sounds do    not sing but
stretch    space to a sm    ear of sil

ence we    as our boots are g    ripped-sc
ratched by bracken can't    hear here or

there    but at least we    just    feel an

edge of silence sli    cing fairy    tales as
hun    ched oaks reach    to    wards our

shapes by being    totally still we    re
lish our in    tru    sion through our minds

and a painting    our brains do    to ground
to make    land    scape's e    scapes

•

we leave    a wide Der
went to flow a    way

from us qui    etly
through    dark we

gently climb park
land towards Eden

sor's spire Lin    dup
Low is allowed to a

public crossed by
an un    fenced B6012

and    in a dark this r
oad rivers headlight

-noise we know    we
will find diffi    cult to

cross Chats    worth
Ho    use is lit

cool blue like    a
digital    copy of its day

time self on    an
horizon a    stag silhou

ette turns    his
head moment    arily

entang    ling his antlers
with bran    ches printed

clear    & black against
sky sun    has just left

# Slake

## *I. Skin Dip*

segments of water     -mesh  ripple    where wind wears     inter
spersed with smooth     see    through sleek eye   -parts     lake takes
my shape even    whilst the bank    holds    on to my foot bones

mud mouths suck    each silent    under surface squelch    is a
footstep through a lewd sentence I wave    invites to your    eyes
so you dare your soles to the earth's    soup of imagined    horror

wriggles    our shapes slake    thirst on black underwater    smoke
the smell    of ditch slicks our skins as a    clearcloak of water
rises & wraps around our    throats    your body is a wave    ring

flag in a wind of wet    touch    your limbs are streamers    ghost
like whilst your solid head pokes in    to a breathable world summer
willows are all speeches stitched green & fishily quivering vis

ions reflected the    sun's    shattered phonemes gleam    as bits of
day condensed on wavelet crests    my head pro    seeds through bob
bing light-blue-bright hyphens of    damsel fly flotillas the    shrish

of breeeze through    reeds is a reading done by some god of a novel
he/she has    written for water whilst    I swim    gentle & delicate
ringing-glugs of surface against    my chin & neck is    anything

but poetry I am naked with    doubts about the safety of my penis    I
slip through a warm layer close to air o    but below    when I let my
legs dangle    in some feminine    way    that's dark i    feel    cold

crystal flowing    i/I    feel    depths hold    eyes    loosening    my
erection    this lake's text runs sub    merged sighlance    a shout
jumps from your    mouth    a fattened sky-trout among swifts & swall

ows swallowing the    vast    alpha    bet of this lake's flies


*II. Skinned Drops*

segments with even    suck
through dare    wriggle smell

and wrap wind whilst willows
reflect condensed light    breeze

she/he glugs poetry through dangle
flowing    *this*    from swallowing

•


ripple through bank
silent sentence    earth's

thirst skins throats

touch pokes stitched
shattered crests of

reading whilst against doubts
air-ways hold merged sky-bets

•

mesh see whilst
each lewd soul

shapes ditch around
wet solid speeches

sun's wavelet hyphens
reeds for surface

faces offshore read
naked    warm some I-lake's

mouth    vast

•

water smooth even
suck through your our

of around wind
your all the on blue

through written of am
through in    i    this from

your wallowing

•

segments disperse
my mud footsteps

so wriggles rise
as flags like willow's

visions day brings
of he/she ringing

but slip lets
crystal erection

jump ow!

•

where sleek holds under wave
soup-black-clear    is streamers

breathable fishy gleams    seeds
flotillas    some gentle neck    safety

below dark loosening silence among this

•

wear parts    feet
squelch your imagined

underwater cloak    wave
ghost    world quivering

as through the    god & is
of when    feel my shout

swifts    flies

•

inter-take bones
an eye's horror

smoke    water    ring
ghost summer visions

of novel delicate anything
i my cold    *my*

shout swallows flies

•


wind-eye on surface invites
underwater clear body

limbs to green phonemes
headed damsel by swim

o that's eyes    merged trout bet

•


layer feminine feel
text mouth vast

surface with close
depths runs

fattened α

fish hush

## Two Llynnau, Moelwynion

### *Llyn yr Arddu*

clasp lasts on the hill    side tent pit    ched amongst heath
er & bracken side    of smile clings to l    andscape's old
haste faint    smoke-pin    ks of heather-f    lowers    light

fad    ing to granu    lar the lock    of the sun clinks its heat
down onto a hidden lake    three    little youth    ful spruces
accomp    any us    and on a toe of rock a row    an    testing

the wind    less gloss of a    llyn we wish to undo    ourselves
by going    in    to the land's hole    gloss    of the llyn the    g
loss perfectly planed    by gravity a spirit    -level bub    ble

amongst craglet-spattered undu    lation we wish to    pick
out a code and be accepted in    to the tight se    crets of wide
plain dropped like rucked    cloth clouds fr    ail a    way and

the moon in    flates its edge from a crag    side some say we
are crimi    nal to break &    enter the moon un    buckles ground
flings lit-grey ghosts' clothing we    must steal our souls from

a box of a    world the moon    herding dark shadows amongst
pewter heather steel    knolls our feet pres    sing among black
bog-wet of this bleeding August until we go    in into our tent to

sleep c    lose to watery gl    oss & brut    ally gentle slosh slosh

## Llyn y Biswail

English are we    criminal to enter &    break    in the lap
of a knight a length of dull    -gleam the llyn under Cnicht

wind cringing on watery skin but we    must steal our bodies
from the world's box and re    place the fakes with love in

the clear llyn-flesh colonies of long green reeds wavering in
one direction    it seems    a language is being    learned or de

livered by a dance of plants lucid    green undulating in dull
clarity as we    pitch our tent with its little footprint near this

engine of codes given    for nothing or no    one and we    let
weather's wet blasts bounce our tent's fabric as the    llyn's

skin    rucks and fish    huddle in the bott    om of some
where imagined we    huddle in our tent like dolls in a run

ning giant's    pocket the long    llyn under Cnicht crin    kles
motion as no    tion pours from a back    log through a narrow

rock channel    flows that bird I bet    that's a raven that bird
pain    ting its f    light onto sky's dim cloud-gloss that    bird

is not theft

## Mortals Through Gogarth

be    lay life hold    her line I    placed
as gar    goyle or an    gel gut    tering at

tention or is it p    raying South
Stack's light    house pokes    out
from behind out    from a side

of a sm    all    conical mountain head
land head    land hung on    sea whit

est tin    foil-like but fluid in    stant crink
led elec    tric    glass-lensed light here
& gone like    one    tick proj

ected from a clock    gapped age    less
until again tiny    bright p

rick through grey    time & grey
space I'm tied    to quart    zite via ny
lon & alloy I    belay pay    out some thin

continuous cur    rency of ropes as she
climbs above    me I am    framed by

ridge & arête in a    niche at my    back
vertical ground    landedge ho    riz
on    tally deep & o    paque in    front

of me a st    upendous  drop of sea
's horizontal    terror-clear-calm sea's

grey-gleam film all jiggling crozzle as is
quartzite's craze    so ever so    slightly
trans    lucent rip    pling sea-like still

ness close    up to my face there    sea so
lidity sea's    solidities solidities'    seas Go

garth's rock syst    ems & structures multi
ply & div    ide fractals of fear-peace geo
logically written as real    imagined

fingers pro    liferate in    cracks touch
ings of hands    on stone pass on    knu

ckles lich    en fingerprints & salt to hist
ories' now-passed nows    (c)limbing guide
book writers die in each    other's mouths

en    chained & on    written cliffs of each
other's pages in space st    retched between

rock to my left to my right in my    crack
of frame a raven    hangs flagly black up
draft-frilled    shocked *crock!* ruck

on air    as speckled-cream-blue-flare
of feather & talons cling-tumbles-attack

peregrine & raven s    pin    and a l    imp
broken meaty sc    rap of pere
grine chick escapes crack    -like shapes

of raven c    laws to fall to    lost my
frame refers empty as instant is

a never now    is only    salted air & airy
seaish    distances(') deaths are a    live
as flight soon    I will untie

nylon knots (untie nyl    on from oil
from age    -compressed es    sence of in

sects) un    tie    from deep ground shout
from throat through mouth through air
through love to    her through her

        "climbing!"

Note: *Gogarth* is the name of a tall and extensive area of sea-cliffs on
Holyhead Island, between South Stack and North Stack. It is a major
climbing venue. The Welsh name *Gogarth* incorporates the following
definitions: promontory, hill, highland, enclosure, step, ledge, terrace.

## Mont Blanc Away

a sky has cryst    alised a solid glare-    white
arc dark    angles & stripes of an air    above

green brown alps screes pines ravines    a rucked
bed a white black-    streaked dream flees an

other air esc    apes to blue    on white's    raz
or    airground    appears through    disappearance

peers    through sense shocks    across crushed

dist

## On Blhà Bienn, Skye, January 1st 2002
### for Nikki & Chris

now snow has no    foot    prints but our    own
after    noon light a gold    for    ever    plating

silver    instant    jagged Black    Cuillin miles
off amongst cloud in    flated by sun    breath

all    dangers of a lifetime    collected laid    out
as black back    bone terrible &    beauty    full

Bl    ack Cuill    in crinkled    silver seen through
wind-thrust spark    ling snow specks ang    er

patient as glaciation sheet    steel-stone bitten and
bent by    some heav    en's sky    blue edge sun

lays light    years of distance    across a rusted
sword an ero    ded vibrance    spindrift l    ays

                glitter across our

faces    glinting ice    -clogged lo    chans cling
amongst a p    ile of planet-sp    linters people call

Black    Cuillin Black    Cuillin Skye's smashed
plough    -blade now    turns thickening air's pur

ple & gr  ey ground    over world    leaks
through sky-rip into vast    black behind every

thing a moon-    drop of frost's    blood touches
and just    balances    on a motion    less tremble

of ragged at    om-narrow horizon    now snow
has no footprints but our    own an    untrodden-

on day    ours to write our    pass    age acro    ss
sssssssssssssssssssssssssssssssssssssssssssssssssssssssssssss

## Peop Tor Ridon Led

scree's tuate spears
white silvery
with black east fingers

our us stone

rocks low with
a we map
punc frozen
tangling of slabs
wriggles cellophane

our invades

wraps winter's
iced hol steps
dim people slender

but

## Dawlish Corner

be in a geo    metry of being on a lip    tucked
coastal corner through    d    ark we daw    dle in

ever    closed d    oor of a corner's o    pen    a black
hole in stacked packed red desert sand    steel

lines plummet in    to corner's beyond    wheeled
boxes of lights ringing a rails' conveying strange

rs' fi    gures & fa    ces passing thro    ugh a rub
of dimension a strip    of a stony beach be    side

a strip of a    rail    way line a tongue    of old sea
-thrown stones & a pal    ate of big-b    locked sea

-wall sea-ex    panse presses lines tight to red
cliffs a darkn    ess presses a red    of a mudstone

towards b    lack & a corner where a head    land
bodies up a Par    son & Clerk cut    off retreat or

proceeding except for fine filaments of steel that
fall horizontally into a Victorian    hole passing

through a fab    ric of ancient desert a black hole
in a stacked packed-hard red mud a    dark daw

a cluttle & crun    ch of feet on peb    bles & crus
hed shells moon    on sea    water a path of milk to

beyond all corners Jesus' feet    feel solid milk to
away but we    could only swim a ch    ill-g    litter

as clouds rip a    part & close a
gain stars make shrills    glinting stones

& shell-specks just    like snow-gleams in moon
light whee    zing limpets make rocks hiss feel    as

if feel ish    feel as if a beach is    hunting us-me-you
with microscopic hunger abundant in wheeze our at

omicstructurescoulddisintegrateinthissoundtobeutter
ly inter    grated beyond a dark air    sings drain-pun

gent sh    apes into your    head via tunnels into your
face speak    into a cliff-acoustic feel    (y)our voice

hung above you on wirey    molecular links push
-pul    ling close & far    meadow grass ordinary

long meadow grass but hanging not standing trans
muted into jungle-ish cur    tains of dangerous lush

meadow grass dan    gling in fringes in dark dripping
cliff's red-black bulk furred in blackened emerald as

a breeze shims through    strands an ancient
giant desert torso of    dead red dust breathes

darkness wemeyou    are    corn    ered but I spot
a wrinkle in un    iverse I    you-us spot

a window-hole a little    oily gleam-disc    seawater
amongst stone clots wiggling a white-lit b    lob of

moon act    ually two moons if you    sway gently as
blackness wraps you letting you(r) lines of vision pass

across a little pool black    & at once (l)it & b(l)ack
again as    one moon rises from one    (one) pool edge

and sets in    an opposite edge at exact    ly a moment
another moon rises where a    first first rose    (pos

sib(y)le    to time it to see two    moons pool
-refl    ected at    once) double

vision un    less one eye is closed so    a lay
ering of places then fails rails    side by side slide ex

   press into a    mouth-eye    of a corner's face

**Ish Coast Etched**

## Zennor Sky

translucent purple-pink Guernsey cows graze
lit silver grass
Zennor sky smashed to pieces on meadow
at forty thousand feet a Cornish coast etched
in steam moments
mermaid-scale-whispers
soft granite out crops
ancestor ash tree living in through & round
a ruined cottage of sky's gold oranges & silver streamers
a sky's insides inside a gurnard's guts
a vast pub of coloured gusts & mist musicians jamming
cumuli-guitars cirrus-chords voices accordion-anvils
buttery sky-milk dribbles twilight
mines plummet deep through heaven's rippling ringing
tin song gone

## On The Zennor Field Path, A West Penwith

### *Ancestor Cottage*

an ash    tree has taken a    way the    glass the roof    vapour
ised in    time the floor    is d    irt tw    igs    & leaves and    the
plaster coils in    shapes of sky & children's    graffiti the alder

sitting at the    table creeks in    to a meal    of years the ivy
dangling from the ash tree    beams just touches    the ground and

        connects    nothing to the    sky


### *Hollow Cottage*

home sucked    out stone-work green
plaster contour    swirled ivy    is

mullions for one    window and wind
is the ever    passing glass of an    other each

bird that comes    here knows
nothing of who    went

## Hollow Ancestor

an ash tree has    taken    away the glass the roof
vaporised in time hollow    cottage the floor home

sucked out is dirt    twigs & leaves stone    work
and the    plaster green    coils plaster in shapes

of sky contour    swirled & child    ren's graffiti ivy
is mullions for one    wind    ow the wind the elder

is the ever pas    sing glass sit    ting at the table
of another creeks    into a meal of years each

bird the ivy that comes here    dangling from the knows
nothing ash tree    beams of who    went    the fox that

past last night just    touches the ground and connects
nothing is red to the sky is the last thought

# On The Zennor Field Path, A West Penwith II

*Ancestor Cottage*

an ash tree
has taken away the glass

the roof
vaporised in time

the floor

is dirt
twigs & leaves

and the plaster
coils

in shapes of sky

& children's graffiti


the alder
sitting at the table
creaks

into a meal

of years

the ivy

dangling from the ash-tree beams



just touches the ground

and connects nothing
to the sky



*Hollow Cottage*

home sucked out

stonework
green

plaster
contour-swirled

ivy
is mullions
for one window

and wind
is the ever-passing glass

of another




each bird
that comes here

knows nothing

of who




went

## Hollow Ancestor

an ash tree
has taken away the glass

the roof
vaporised in time hollow cottage

the floor
home sucked out is dirt twigs & leaves

stone-work
and the plaster
green
coils

plaster
in shapes
of sky
contour-swirled
& children's graffiti

ivy
is mullions
for one window

the wind

the elder
is the ever passing glass
sitting at the table
of another

creaks
into a meal
of years

each bird
the ivy that comes here
dangling from the knows nothing
ash tree beams
of who

went

the fox
that passed last night just touches the ground
and connects
nothing is red
to the sky

is the last thought

Note: *Ancestor Cottage II* & *Hollow Cottage II* are transcriptions
of an improvisation audio-recorded on location.

*Hollow Ancestor II* is a transcription
of an audio-mix of the live improvisations.

## Zy Nor Sken

trans lit on ish
scale ash of

insides coloured
guitars sky through

merm met deep

lucent grass ow!
etched wisps

living gold inside

gusts cirrus
dribbles heavens'

pink sky thousand

in stream granite
round silver guts

musicians' voices

mines ringing
cows graze to peace

a corn mermaid

or age a sky's
pub of cumuli

buttery met
deep gone

## Passing Through Sea-Thorn

sheets of salt    -light slice    frontal
greys land to our    backs sea    to our faces

a little    vill    age of Rinsey    & its pure
wet name behind    our minds clings to a slip

pery tilt of world    as angered January tugs
at it & us    with bur    sting sky Rinse

y at a    back of land our feet    fed across vague
at a back of a coast's    dumb mouth

as ocean shouts deep backlogs of vast    rain
trick    ling a    long thorns    a taut

fraying r    ope of coast    -path pass    es through
a purple-black blackthorn cloud    thorn-

clitt-clatt    wind shreds through sharp wood
a wren's frag    ment wrapped in brown

glimpse    Rinsey Head's sing    le howled-at
house tightening distances round its gran    ite

selfness teet    ering fast on a cl    iff-lip facing
sea's visible sizzling voices & s    pray's

seen scraping phrases & wind's    ever
uttered touches    contains deep indoors    a floor

-corner with warm    still fluff    no one has
touched    blackthorn's long inter    laced pricks

a mesh of weapon    ry ranks    of skeletal
fretting either    side of footworn hawser-width

clickt-drip clackt-drop thorn    phantoms
shudder under wind    -strings I am spine on

femurs & shins myself strung to    jolts wind
grinds my brow each boot    -clunk disconnects

me to path-pebbles and    thence to sol
id but erodable    depth a bag    of air bursts a burden

of spatters a wet    hammering holly leaves
glisten-rattle    gorse in bloom with boun    cing

golden scraps is a hill    side of dancing ram
blers clad    in gaudy yellow Gore

-tex jackets heat    & moisture leak from joints
in my high    -tech shell    sweat wicks    up through

a finely woven mesh of syn    the    tic fibres    Praa
Sands rushed    by ringing    froth & curling

shrouds of ocean skimming    scum-foam like
weightless bread sliding sideways    a figure

& his/her spring    er on sand    faint & miniature
at a weather's far    end be    yond behind

this human's & dog's    minds houses    flat
white wet paper squares balanced    on an

old eroding rim bet    ween a thick depth of    sea
& heavy    height    of sky all    impossibly not

        b    lown a    way su    ggests

Note: Praa is pronounced as 'pray' (or perhaps 'prair');
it should not be pronounced as 'Prare'.    eɪ    ɛ:    ɑ:

## Aromomentic Lo(r)cation, Andaluvia

planet-old plat    eau(-)built from time's    a
roma land    scape pushed through a bull's no

strils stone    smeared on my finger    prints
volatile rosemary per    formed upon by wind

& water    sinuous    sweet stinging medium sea
-bed micro-bones    & muscles of youths stretched

through soft hot torture    a cabra    monté's sweet
unsayable    memories his horns    weapons el

egant as nostalgia across the valley    from him
light smells as possible as fragmented chess

pieces on the wrecked foot    path females are
flaking look-outs    stunted Classical statues

written through pre    -histories' dimensions wild
crystallizes in the sun    shine I scramble in among

my hat's miniature mountain-range    stain round
my crown of buttresses & thorn    -full slots

I get myself beneath my steps    clonk-rattle jump
an irreversible moment all    the stench collects

on my mask    sweat erodes sierras gleefully    night
rises its loaf without    light frightened among aroma

I clamber    round closed    among neon-purple petals
dark mouths curl fragments of bird    song cold

through pine-needles    my fortieth year's ghostly
blue noise    I hang my meat on one direction's eroded

remains freighted    to be    smelled a small animated
statue annihil    ating wrong worlds with bright weight

less selves    brain maze with a cloud-shadow pass
fold flaps & channels of nostalgia across    a synapse

battling like bandits & fascists dance    I could laugh
some world's limestone plateau in my mouth    hear

grey matter's coppery spread feel    azure's evil iris
rise on a pale green    length of exit    perspective

steps amongst brief flow    ers & human eff    luvia

## Aromatic Sierra Tejeda, Andalucía

planet-old moun    tain    built now    from aroma
eve    n the scene    ry's pulled in    to nostril-like

eyes rose    mary sm    eared on my fingerprints is
volatile & sin    uous sweet stinging threads lime

stone & pine are beautiful    said    sweetest mem
ories of mountains(') muscles    from youth stretch

through past's mag    ma hot soft nost    algia light
smells fragmented & possible on the footpath climb

ing & switch    backing among box    wood olivillo
rowans thorns white beams flaking pines & stunt

ed ever    green oaks    trees written in three    dimen
sions on    to the mountainside like old gods' alpha

bets    sculpted & dropped    through dim    ension
dreamt like fantasy cryst    all    ising in sunshine

mountain pulling    out illness    my back under my
rucksack is sweat-drenched    a me    washing my

self with wet selves    soaked-husk body-shapes wh
iff of in-place my    brimmed hat is stained with a

81

miniature mountain range of my moisture & grease
round my crown I   have leaked    mountain-ness

clonk-rattle of pale pine-sticks beneath my steps I
tread skeleton each    push    with each    foot up

collects all    the stench & perfumes of my frame
& ghost to one    moment of motion on    ground

odorous all the Sierra Tejeda rises as    one mass
ive ancient loaf of bread seen    from the rich

tomato & artichoke plain of Zafarraya through
haze grey screes & grey-green trees mottle/stripe

earth upthrust to the sum    mit of Maroma    I am
in this distance un    seen amongst aromas this year

rain has fattened spring ringing    greens yellow
-blooms chime    mountain cherry oregano hedgehog

broom columbine milk vetch mountain crucifer sax
ifrage thyme toadflax lavender    quick lime-juicy

streaks of    lizard between    rocks creamy clusters
of crisp flowers tinsel-rattle a platinum    centipede

curled among neon    -purple petals    glaring &
dappled lime-gravel dry stream-bed where winter's

waters    present gone    sonic    fragrances of bird
song    robin rock bunting blue rock thrush crag

martin wood    pecker-laugh-hammering    hawk
whistle &    wheesh    -constant of breeze through

pine-needles and a    round cones' wooden gongs
noise    ghostly blue as The Med far below eroding

Malaga's coast but not    a back-&-forth wish-hush
of surf    just    one long wish of wind in one    di

rection its freight to    be smelled    annihilating
wrong worlds with bright    weightless solid dark

arrow-mania cloud    -shadows pass across crags
above me and spill    down gorge-walls below    are

truth & nostalgia battling like    bandits & fascists
making a seen    -gleeful (st)ink of laughter I could

laugh pop    a limestone pebble into my    mouth
phero    mone-bread-stone aro    matic nougat of

energy sweat's    sweet-salt-hiss in my eye-nose um
ber & zing of cru    shed juniper berry between poin

ting finger &    thumb the hum    ming paste of my
coppery human turd spread amongst pine-needles to

dry in the sun    ef    flu    via

## Voltage

willow stitched into evening sky    black veins
& fish    jacket of dimensions    woven living ink

complex dark hand on smooth blue skin
skin deep as every thing    as very where    owl call

expands droplets of dew    my tongue runs round
my mouth    feels slippery teeth & soft lip-skin

I feel in dark    pink    a cloud builds a white house
full of blackening dream & dazzling tendrils

willow's soft bending knives slicing coming night's
vast blue mind    I run my tongue round my mouth

imagine my teeth & jawbone dry    very thing    my tongue
rotted gone    gone long ago    a smell from soil rises

coils its touch round my brain's naked tip    rain trembles
unfallen    my throat's bulb glows sound    willow-lattice

entwined with world & where    roots spook through ground
leaves shuffle laden air    my red lattice of veins vibrates

up from feet to skull life jolts

## Star Frost, A Corie Làir, A Strath Carron

hill-framed    sky's    cloud
less bl    ue pinks    at its
rim as day's    ghost be

comes    becomes    towards
real becomes and    fills
world our fingers scor    ch

on boot la    ces & gaiter zips
we are cr    isp between Chri
stmas & New Year's Eve our

old    selves suddenly spec
tres of some    others in
nocent of    everything other

than    this this    year-end mist
has    wrapped birch twigs hea
ther & rocks with lit grey splin

ters the burn rum    mages un
der skins    of ice pat    iently sear
ching for    gravity pines    wear

frilly jackets of white sky-breath
and one pine    stop    -framed by
hun    dreds of its still likes walks

with   us star-prongs   have gr
own over every High   land detail
of   here here   recreated as cry

stalline copies of fo   rest &
corie & mountains beyond   this
breath   ing & passing   of our

selves through this per   fectly new
world is a yoga of   ground ground
takes us in   to its star shapes   a

robin stops bobs stops bobs be
fore   us leading us   up a
slippery footpath each   bootfall

crinks against master   piece ice
-broaches tra   gically but for bil
lions up   on billions of tiny

delicate sym   metrical shapes wa
ter's spoken has frozen to we   go
to   beyond beyond   the tree

-line high &   out in   the open ice
-wires nest in   our noses as we
breathe ourselves towards Corie Làir

& Sgor Rhaudh ri   zing above
the corie's grey frost   -base to frisp
golden rid   ges of crystal   line

desire where sunlight cracks & cra
shes si   lently speckly   -white ptar
migan are invisible but   they are

there and they see    with frost's
eyes night's veins waiting just
below a world's    rim darkness just

lea    king in and free    sing
into this    bright we are warm    as
our bones burn    like frost I want

to stay

still in this    high light stay
here as a solid vow
el    a crystal man    an

an

# Acknowledgements

Thank you to the following magazines and their editors for first publishing (or accepting for publication) poems from this collection: *Cleaves, Fire, Gists and Piths, Litter, Poetry Wales, Shearsman, Stride Magazine.*

Thank you to *Arts in The Peak* for first publishing part of 'Moor on Paper Under Foot'.

'Distance a Sudden' was first published as a pamphlet, a handmade chapbook, and an audio CD by Longbarrow Press. A CD audio version of Ish Coast Etched was also first published by Longbarrow Press.

Thank you to Brian Lewis for his audio mix which, in this collection, has been transcribed and entitled *Hollow Ancestor II*.

Thank you for encouragement and/or critical comments from: Alan Baker, Elizabeth-Jane Burnett, Matt Clegg, Kerry Featherstone, Tony Frazer, John Gallas, Andy Hirst, members of Inky Fish, Chris Jones, Brian Lewis, Robert Macfarlane, Chris Mitchell, Austin Orwin, Harriet Tarlo.

Thank you to Tim Allen for his close reading of the entire manuscript.

Thank you to Julia Thornley for her intensely close reading and precise proofing of the text(s). Also thanks for her openness towards my poetic procedure, and her incisive critical questioning which has made a vital creative contribution to this book.

Thank you to Tony Frazer for his careful and creative physical design of this book, which has become an integral part of what *Back of A Vast* attempts to express.

Cover photo: detail taken from a photograph by Nikki Clayton, entitled *Black Cuillin from Sands*. Ish Coast Etched photo: by Nikki Clayton, entitled *Plaster-Swirl, Zennor Coast Path*.

Thank you to climbing and mountain walking partners: Lisa Claxton, Nikki Clayton, Chris & Jonny Mitchell, Boz Morris.

Thank you to Nikki for being my companion in many places and in all kinds of weather, and for her close attention to *Back of A Vast*.

Lightning Source UK Ltd.
Milton Keynes UK
UKOW050620160312

189062UK00001B/37/P